ublished by
ederation of Family
istory Societies
Publications) Ltd.
nits 15-16
nesham Industrial Centre
ram Street, Bury
ancs BL9 6EN
nited Kingdom

BN 1-86006-185-0

irst published 2005

Printed and bound by
The Alden Press
Osney Mead
Oxford OX2 OEF

Methodist Records
for
Family Historians

Richard Ratcliffe

SERIES EDITOR
Pauline M. Litton

CONTENTS

HISTORY AND ORGANISATION

(a) JOHN WESLEY

The Methodist movement was born at Oxford University in November 1729. A small group of students, which included John Wesley, Fellow of Lincoln College and son of the Rev. Samuel Wesley of Epworth in Lincolnshire and his wife Susannah [nee Annesley], formed a Society, which became known as the "Bible Moths" or "Methodists" because of their methodical and austere way of life, their daily bible study and prayer meetings. After graduating in Divinity and Classics in 1724, and qualifying for his M.A. in 1725, John became a deacon of the Church of England in 1726 and was elected Fellow of Lincoln College in 1727, qualifying him to become a teacher and lecturer, a post which he took up there in 1729. After a disastrous two years as a missionary and chaplain in Georgia in America from 1735-1737, John returned to England in a very depressed state in February 1737/8. On May 24th 1738, John attended a meeting of the Moravian Society (a German Protestant group) in Aldersgate Street, London where "At about a quarter to nine, I felt my heart strangely warmed. I felt I did trust in Christ, Christ alone for salvation, and an assurance was given me, that he had taken away my sins, even mine and saved me from the law of sin and death." From that moment onwards he set out to revive the Church of England, reform the Poor Law and the Penal Code, abolish slavery, improve conditions in the prisons and stop the exploitation of labour in the factories and mines.

(b) WESLEY AND WHITEFIELD

Initially John Wesley was supported and encouraged by George Whitefield, but by 1741 the two men and their followers had fallen out over their differing interpretations of the Gospel. Whitefield supported the Calvinist Doctrine of Predestination, while Wesley favoured the Arminian Doctrine of Justification by Faith. Although the two men remained on cordial terms right up to Whitefield's death in 1770, Wesley was to encourage his followers to build chapels or preaching houses, while Whitefield's followers built tabernacles in which they held their preaching services. Many of Whitefield's tabernacles eventually became Congregational Churches (in England), but those in Wales became Calvinist Methodist Chapels, remaining as part of the Anglican Church until 1811 before breaking away to form the Presbyterian Church of Wales.

(c) DEVELOPMENT OF THE METHODIST MOVEMENT 1739 – 1791

Between 1739 and his death in 1791, Wesley travelled the length and breadth of the British Isles and was especially effective as a preacher in London, Cornwall, Yorkshire and the industrial centres of Bristol, Manchester and Birmingham. He is said to have travelled 250,000 miles on horseback and preached 40,000 sermons in his 52 years' ministry. By the time of his death on March 2nd 1791 at the age of 88, there were a considerable number of Methodists within the Church of England. Wesley's "Journal" - his diary of his travels, meetings and services – is one of the major autobiographies of the 18th Century.

In 1739, Wesley built the New Room Chapel in the Horsefair in Bristol, which became his headquarters in the West of England. He laid the foundation stone on May 12th 1739, only five weeks after preaching his first open air service in Bristol, and opened it for public worship on June 3rd. Wesley spent more time in the New Room than any other place during the next 50 years. Here he wrote hundreds of letters and many of his books, including his 'Primitive Physick', a book of remedies. It was here that he trained his travelling preachers and in 1742 started the Methodist Class meetings – the bedrock of Methodism. Here in 1771 he commissioned Francis Asbury to go to America as a missionary where he became the founding father of American Methodism and the first

Bishop of the Methodist Episcopal Church in 1784. It was near the New Room where John Wesley's younger brother Charles lived at 4 Charles Street, Bristol from 1749-1771 and where he wrote many of his 6,000 hymns.

In the same year, 1739, John Wesley bought the remains of the Old Foundery in Moorfields, just outside the City of London, refurbished it and made it his London headquarters until he replaced it in 1779 with a new chapel 'in nearby City Road. The Foundery was more than a Chapel — it was a free dispensary, a school for pauper children, an almshouse for widows and a lending bank to help people get started in business.

In 1744, Wesley held the first of the Annual Conferences in the Foundery. These were meetings of his helpers, to confer with them on the doctrines, and on the disciplines, which they should exercise, as well as to decide where his preachers should be stationed. Following each Annual Conference, the Minutes of Conference are published and they are a valuable source of Methodist history and biography.

In 1783, the Methodist Conference persuaded Wesley to ordain preachers to go to America where ordained ministers were urgently needed. He did so reluctantly but refused to ordain ministers in this country who wished to administer the Sacraments. As he was seeking to revive the Church of England, he urged Methodists to continue to receive Holy Communion in their parish churches.

(d) DIVISIONS WITHIN METHODISM 1791 – 1932

Within five years of Wesley's death in 1791, the Wesleyan Movement had effectively broken away from the Church of England and had become the Wesleyan Methodist Church.

Several groups, all of which retained the name Methodist, broke away from Wesley's Church.

The first group, led by Alexander Kilham [who was also born in Epworth] broke away in 1797 to form the METHODIST NEW CONNEXION (MNC).

The MNC came into being on August 9th 1797, when Alexander Kilham, William Thom, Stephen Eversfield and Alexander Cummin met at the Ebenezer Chapel in Leeds and formally set up the MNC. This was as a result of the refusal of the Wesleyan Conference to discuss the times of Sunday services, and to appoint laymen to share in the administration of the Church at Circuit and District Meetings and at the Annual Conference. The MNC quickly took root in the North of England and by 1847, its Golden Jubilee year, the MNC had 20,000 members in the UK, 30,000 members in Canada, 141 ministers, 334 chapels and 38,000 Sunday School scholars.

The second group to break away from the Wesleyans, in 1807, were the PRIMITIVE METHODISTS led by Hugh Bourne who was born at Fordhays Farm, near Stoke on Trent, and William Clowes a relative of Josiah Wedgwood. Bourne and Clowes were two Wesleyan ministers who wanted to bring about a religious revival in the Potteries and mining villages of North Staffordshire. Holding open air 'Camp Meetings' at Mow Cop near Tunstall, Staffordshire, many people were converted but their membership was not recognised by the Wesleyan Conference. The name Primitive Methodist comes from an address by John Wesley to his preachers in Chester in 1790, "Go out into the streets and lanes of the city and bring in the poor, the maimed, the halt and the blind and this is the way the Primitive Methodists did."

The Primitive Methodists, nicknamed "the Ranters" because of their singing in the streets, soon spread into Nottinghamshire, Lincolnshire, Liverpool, West Yorkshire, East Anglia and Essex and later into Cornwall and South Wales. In 1849 the PM Conference recorded a membership of 104,762, with 519 ministers, 8,524 local preachers and 5,170 chapels.

3

The third breakaway group were the BIBLE CHRISTIANS. They came into being in Cornwall in 1815. William O'Bryan, a Wesleyan Local Preacher who had earlier been rejected as a candidate for the Wesleyan Ministry, held a preaching service at Lake Farm, Shebbear on October 9th 1815 and enrolled 22 members, who became known locally in Cornwall as Free Willers, Shining Lights and Bryanites. The Bible Christians grew apace and by 1865, when they celebrated their Golden Jubilee in Exeter, they reported 750 Chapels, 2,000 Ministers and local Preachers, 26,000 members, 40,000 Sunday School scholars and 8,000 Sunday School teachers.

Other breakaway groups include the Protestant Methodists, the Wesleyan Methodist Association and the Wesleyan Reformers. The last three groups amalgamated in 1857 to form the UNITED METHODIST FREE CHURCH (UMFC). At that time the UMFC had a membership of 40,000, 110 ministers and 769 chapels.

In the meantime, the original WESLEYAN METHODIST CHURCH had been making many important changes, such as allocating places at the Annual Conference and at District Meetings to laymen, making Wesley's travelling preachers "ministers" after a four year probationary period, and also giving them authority to administer Holy Communion or the Sacrament of the Lord's Supper. In 1818 the use of the prefix "Reverend" was authorised.

Moves to unite Methodism proceeded very slowly following initial overtures being made by the Methodist New Connexion to the Wesleyan Conference of 1866.

In 1907, the United Methodist Free Church, the Methodist New Connexion and the Bible Christians agreed to form the UNITED METHODIST CHURCH.

(e) UNITY IN 1932 AND
   ORGANISATION

Finally in 1932, the United Methodist Church, the Primitive Methodist Church and the Wesleyan Methodist Church came together and formed the METHODIST CHURCH, which has become the much slimmer Methodist Church of today.

Amalgamation of the administration of the different groups of Methodism was comparatively easy as each group followed the lines of administration devised by John Wesley at the first Conference of 1744. Wesley set out clear lines of communication within the Methodist movement, which are still basically the same today.

There is the ANNUAL CONFERENCE [or Assembly] which is the principal decision making body — it also confirms the stationing of ministers for the coming church year. It is now composed of the Chairmen of each of the Districts plus elected ministers and laypersons from each District.

Under the Conference are the Districts, covering several counties in most cases and made up of a large number of Circuits who are answerable to the Chairman of the District.

The half-yearly SYNODS of the DISTRICTS implement decisions taken by the Conference, consider reports from national and district committees, and discuss responses to go back to the next Conference as well as electing their representatives to go to Conference.

Each District is divided into a number of Circuits. A circuit is a group of chapels overseen by a Superintendent Minister

The Quarterly meetings of the CIRCUITS implement decisions taken by Conference and passed on from the District Synods. They elect representatives to attend their District Synod; and discuss Circuit matters, some of which may be referred to the District Synod or possibly to Conference.

Each Chapel within a Circuit also holds meetings every three months to receive information passed down from the Circuit meetings and District Synods and to discuss responses that may be required by these bodies as well as dealing with Chapel matters.

4

These Quarterly meetings are now called Church Council meetings but were formerly called Trustees' Meetings or Leaders' Meetings.

All these meetings, and the many committees which feed into them, have produced a mass of documents over the past 260 years, many of which may be of interest to family historians.

LOCAL METHODIST CHAPEL RECORDS – BAPTISMAL REGISTERS

The early Methodists began to build preaching houses in the 1760s and children of Methodists soon began to be baptised in these meeting places. Few Baptismal Registers survive before 1790 and most children of early Methodists continued to be baptised in the Church of England. After 1800 the practice of Infant Baptism in Methodist Chapels became more common. In 1812, The Wesleyan Methodist Conference urged churches to register Baptisms.

"1. Let that ordinance, if possible, be always administered in the public congregation.

2. Let us administer it, in general, only to the children of our members and those of our regular hearers.

3. Let a small fee be taken for registering Baptisms where the parents can afford to pay it; let such fees after defraying the expense of the register Book be given to the poor."

Soon after the introduction of Civil Registration of Births, Marriages and Deaths in July 1837, the Non-Parochial Registers Act required all Methodist Chapels [and other Nonconformist Chapels] to deposit their pre – 1837 registers with the Registrar-General. 856 volumes from all branches of Methodism were deposited. Microfilmed copies can be seen at the Family Records Centre [FRC] in London in Class RG4. They have also been microfilmed by the Genealogical Society of Utah [GSU], are widely available elsewhere in County Record Offices and Family History Centres of the Church of Jesus Christ of Latter-Day Saints as well as in the International Genealogical Index and familysearch website of the GSU. A listing of all 856 registers by County is included in William Leary's book "My Ancestors were Methodists" [Third Edition] published by the Society of Genealogists in 1999.

Before depositing these registers, some ministers made a copy of the register entries. These may now be found in the custody of the present Circuit Superintendent Minister or in the nearest County Record Office [CRO] or Archives Office.

The Beverley Wesleyan Circuit Baptismal Register 1827-1876, deposited at the East Yorkshire Archives Office in Beverley, opens with this entry: "The entries from No 1 to No 37 inclusive are copies, the originals of which were forwarded to London to the Registration Commissioners on the 13th July 1837 by me J. Stephenson."

Since 1837, Methodist Baptismal Registers have been kept by the Minister of the Church. There are two kinds of Baptismal Register which may survive:

(a) The Circuit Baptismal Register, which contains the names of children baptised in the Circuit. This often includes dates of birth as well as dates of Baptism, and sometimes the mother's Maiden Surname. It is worth noting that many Methodist Circuits ignored County boundaries. For example, Bole [Nottinghamshire] Wesleyan Methodist Chapel was opened in the 1860s but closed in 1950s. Copies of its baptisms can be found in Gainsborough [Lincolnshire] Wesleyan Circuit Registers at Lincolnshire Archives Office as Bole was in the Gainsborough Wesleyan Methodist Circuit even though Bole is in Nottinghamshire.

(b) The local Chapel Baptismal Register begun in 1837/8 may still be in use in the

5

present Chapel. Unfortunately many of these early registers have been lost or are in private hands, such as the families of Chapel officers or local historians, but a large number thankfully can be located in the local CRO, in the Chapel or Circuit safe or even at the Minister's Manse.

Many chapels have been closed since Methodist Union in 1932, especially where earlier there were two or even three chapels in the same town or village. The Baptismal Registers from the closed chapels can often be located in the nearest CRO.

It is well worth checking copies of Kelly's or White's Directories of the 19th Century and early 20th Century to find out what Methodist Chapels existed in a town or village. If there are no records of some of those Chapels in the CRO you should ask the County Archivist to put you in touch with the Methodist Circuit or District Archivist.

LOCAL METHODIST CHAPEL RECORDS – MARRIAGE REGISTERS

The holding of marriages in Methodist Chapels was legalised in 1837, if the chapel obtained a Certificate of Registration, but few chapels initially registered. Many Methodist Chapels did not obtain a Certificate of Registration until many years later and many marriages of Methodist couples continued to take place in Anglican Churches. Where a Chapel was registered, the local Registrar had to attend and record the marriage in his register, which was kept at the Register Office. The Chapel itself did not keep an official marriage register, but some ministers kept "unofficial" registers and, if they survived, these can sometimes be found in CROs, or even among family papers.

The Marriage Act 1898 meant that the attendance of Registrars at marriages in Methodist Chapels was not always necessary as previously. A number of Methodist Ministers were now legally appointed to conduct and register marriages in specified Chapels. Where a Chapel was not registered, the Registrar still had to attend, and this continues to apply today.

Methodist Marriage Registers may be found in two places. Where a Chapel has been closed but was previously registered for marriages, the Register should be located in the CRO. Where the Chapel is still in use and registered, the Marriage Registers are kept by the Minister in the Chapel or Circuit safe. A fee may be chargeable for a search. Please note that these registers are not usually indexed.

LOCAL METHODIST CHAPEL RECORDS – BURIAL REGISTERS

The Wesleyan Methodist Conference in 1803 ordered that a Register of Deaths of members of each Methodist Society should be kept in every Circuit. Very few Registers of Deaths survive. Where Chapels had burial grounds attached, the Burial Registers were surrendered to the Registrar General with the Baptismal Registers in 1840. There were a con-siderable number of such burial grounds in Cheshire, Lancashire and Yorkshire. For most Methodists, their funeral services in the Chapel were followed by interment in the Anglican Churchyard or in the Parish or Town Cemetery. Plans of large Churchyards, burial grounds and Cemeteries often show that they are divided into Anglican, Nonconformist and Roman Catholic burial areas. The Cemetery Burial Register usually records the religious persuasion of the deceased, whereas the Anglican Church Burial Register usually does not. Some Parish Registers do contain comments about the burial of Methodists e.g. Wrangle in Lincolnshire records a number of Methodist burials between 1752 and 1770. Where Methodist burial grounds are still open, and the Chapel is still in use, the Burial Register will be kept by the Minister of the Chapel.

Where the Chapel is closed, the Burial Register should be in the CRO.

The best known Methodist Burial Grounds are at Wesley's Chapel in London, where John Wesley and 5,450 others were buried between 1779 and 1854, and at Englesea Brook near Stoke on Trent, where Hugh Bourne and other early Primitive Methodists are buried.

OTHER LOCAL METHODIST CHAPEL RECORDS

Methodists have always been very conscientious in keeping written records of Chapel meetings and of the many and varied committees within the life of the Chapel. The records of a typical Methodist Chapel dating from the early 19th Century may include some of these records.

◆ **Baptismal Registers** [see above].

◆ **Marriage Registers** [see above].

◆ **Burial Registers** [see above].

◆ **Register of Members/Community Roll/Church Directory.** Many chapels have kept registers from the date of opening to the present day or up to the date of closure of a chapel. These registers usually include the address of a member and may include information about the chapel a member has come from or has moved to, as well as recording the death of a member or in some instances "ceased to meet," or "fallen" where a member has stopped attending the chapel.

◆ **Class Lists and names of Class Leaders.** These are lists of people who were declared members of the church, who used to meet each week for Bible study and prayer at the home of the Class Leader. Members of a chapel are still put in classes but not all classes meet on such a regular basis. Early 19th Century Class Books often give the names of members, their marital status, occupation and address.

◆ **Leaders' Meeting Minutes or Church Council Minutes.** These are the Minute books of chapel members who have been elected to look after the chapel property, the quality of worship in the services and pastoral care for members. The Minute books often show the names of all who attended and are sometimes accompanied by an Attendance Register, which everyone present has signed.

◆ **Annual Chapel Meeting Minute Books.** These contain annual reports from the different organisations in the chapel and the names of chapel officers elected for the following year.

◆ **Society Stewards' Accounts or Chapel Stewards' Accounts.** These show a Chapel's annual income and expenditure. Some are merely summary records, but others are very detailed and informative.

◆ **Collection Journals and Weekly Offering Ledgers.** These books record details of chapel collections and the names of the ministers and local preachers who took the services.

◆ **Pew Rent Records.** Before the Second World War, many chapels were well attended and members paid monthly or quarterly Pew Rents to reserve their seats. They paid different rates depending where they sat in the chapel. From these lists it may be possible to work out where your ancestors sat if the pews haven't been replaced by chairs in recent times.

◆ **Trustees' Minutes and memoranda regarding the Appointment of Trustees.** Every chapel was required to appoint Trustees to be responsible for the upkeep of the chapel buildings. Trustees were often appointed for life. New Trusts were only formed when half of the old Trustees had either died or moved out of the area.

◆ **Sunday School Minutes/ Accounts/ Registers.** Many chapels used to have flourishing Sunday Schools and kept detailed records of scholars' attendances, Anniversary services and outings.

◆ **Choir Minutes.** These often record information about choir members, which

7

parts they sang, special concerts and services as well as disputes between choir members and the organist!

♦ **Building Fund Minutes and Accounts**. These may include information about chapel extensions, fund raising events and names of generous donors.

♦ **Wesley Guild Minutes/Roll book/ Accounts**.

♦ **Band of Hope and Temperance Meeting Minutes/Registers and Accounts**. Band of Hope and Temperance Meetings were held to persuade Chapel Members to abstain from drinking anything alcoholic. Those who 'took the pledge' were given a certificate and these often turn up in collections of family papers.

♦ **Christian Endeavour Meeting Minutes/Register and Accounts**.

♦ **Youth Club Minutes and Accounts**.

♦ **Women's Meeting/ Ladies' Circle Minutes and Accounts**.

♦ **Commemorative Plaques and Memorials**.

Many Chapels contain memorial plaques celebrating the lives of men and women who have served as Trustees, Sunday School Teachers, Organists, etc. The names of generous benefactors are often recorded as are people who laid foundation stones. Look on the outside walls of Chapels if possible. Some have stones bearing the names of all those who contributed towards the building of the Chapel.

RECORDS OF THE METHODIST CIRCUIT

Every Methodist chapel belongs to a Circuit, or used to belong to a circuit before the chapel was closed. A Circuit may comprise only 2 or 3 chapels in some towns and cities but as many as 20-30 chapels in rural areas. Circuit records may include duplicate records of chapels in the circuit as well as records of the different circuit meetings and organisations.

Methodist Circuits often crossed County boundaries so it is worth looking for Chapel and Circuit Records in at least two CROs where a Chapel was built in a village close to a County boundary. For example, the Banbury Circuit includes villages in Northamptonshire, North Oxfordshire and South Warwickshire.

A typical list of Circuit records may include:

♦ **Circuit Registers of Baptisms**. A combined register of baptisms in each of the circuit chapels.

♦ **Preaching Plans and Circuit Directories**. First printed in the late 18th Century and still published by every Circuit to this day, every three to four months. These give details of the names of preachers in the Circuit and where they are appointed to preach. Recent Circuit plans may give details of Officers and Class Leaders in each Chapel in the Circuit. Most County Record Offices have good collections of Preaching Plans as has the Methodist Archives at the John Rylands University Library in Manchester (see page 10 for details). These are often the only printed source of evidence of a person's service to a Chapel or Circuit. 20th Century Plans may include the person's address and telephone number, as well as offices held.

♦ **Circuit Quarterly Meeting Minute Books**. These summarise the business of the circuit and list the names of attendees and those who have given apologies for absence.

♦ **Local Preachers' Meeting Minute Books**. Methodism relies heavily on Local Preachers to conduct services as it has many more chapels than ordained ministers. Local preachers go through a rigorous programme of training before they are "Fully Accredited". The Minute Books record how Local Preachers progress from being "On Note" to being "On Trial" to becoming "Fully Accredited". A large number of young local preachers used then to go forward to train for the Methodist ministry and the Minute books record the support and encouragement they received from the Circuit. There may be a collection of Preachers' Candidating Forms attached to the Minute books in these cases.

◆ **Circuit Property Schedules.** Give information about the condition of each chapel in the circuit. These would have been completed by the chapel stewards and signed by them as well as by the minister chairing the meeting.

◆ **Circuit Registers of Members.** Lists of members attending each of the chapels in the circuit. They also record deaths of members, transfers of membership between chapels and circuits and sadly some who had ceased to be members.

◆ **Circuit Trustees.** Lists of Trustees and Minutes of their meetings. Circuits appointed Trustees and stewards to be responsible for circuit property, especially the Manses in which the ministers lived. Until comparatively recent times the Circuit officers were responsible for furnishing the manses. Some Circuits did this as cheaply as possible as the minutes show.

◆ **Chapel Registration Certificates.** Confirm that the Chapel was a registered place of worship.

◆ **Circuit Accounts.** Include details of expenses incurred when ministers moved to another circuit.

◆ **Circuit Class Books.** List the names of members in each Chapel and to which class they were allocated for spiritual and pastoral care.

◆ **Circuit Account Books.** Show sums of money paid to poor members of the Circuit out of collections taken "for the Poor Fund" at Communion Services, now called the "Benevolent Fund".

◆ **Miscellaneous Records.** Many Circuits have a collection of such records. These may include items such as reports on the Sunday Schools in the Circuit, names of

subscribers to the circuit magazine or to a weekly Methodist newspaper, Trip Books listing names of people who went on Circuit outings and how much they paid, the Horse Hire Fund or Travel Fund accounts showing expenses paid to ministers and local preachers in the days before bicycles and motor cars.

◆ **Chapel Histories.** Many written to celebrate Centenaries, 150th Anniversaries and bi-Centenaries.

Local Newspapers are a rich source of information about Methodist activities in local chapels or of circuit events. There may be reports about Sunday services and weekday meetings, Chapel Anniversaries, Sunday School Anniversaries, Chapel and Sunday School outings, Boys' Brigade and Girls' Brigade activities, Boy Scouts and Girl Guides Company activities, Choir concerts, Circuit Rallies especially the annual celebration of Wesley Day on May 24th, and pen portraits of prominent local worthies some of whom were Methodists.

Census returns available between 1851 and 1901 are another source for locating Methodist ancestry. They record a Minister's occupation as "Wesleyan Methodist Minister" or "Primitive Methodist Minister" and some Local Preachers are recorded as "Farmer and Wesleyan Methodist Local Preacher." In some instances children are recorded as Methodist Sunday School scholars.

The Ecclesiastical Census of 1851, which was taken on Census Sunday, 30th March 1851 is of considerable interest as it gives details of the number of people who attended all Churches and Chapels on that day, as well as the number of Sunday School scholars who attended each place of worship. The complete Ecclesiastical Census can be seen at the National Archives, but County Record Offices and Local Studies Libraries usually hold copies of the Census for their local areas. It is also available on-line at:
enquiry@nationalarchives.gov.uk
or tel: 020 8876 3444.

Many early Methodists kept diaries not dissimilar in many ways to Wesley's Journal. These may be found in County Record Offices or Local Studies Libraries, either in Manuscript form or in published limited editions. These make interesting reading as they mention Chapels and class meetings that the diarists attended and the names of people whom they met or with whom they stayed on their travels.

NATIONAL OR CONNEXIONAL RECORDS OF METHODISM

Records about the District Synods, the Annual Conferences of the Methodist Church, national officers and Departments of the Methodist Church are not usually found in County Record Offices or in other local Repositories. The records are usually known as Connexional Records (or national records).

The largest collection of **Methodist Connexional Records** has been deposited at John Rylands University Library in Manchester. The Methodist Conference of 1961 set up the Methodist Archives and Research Centre [MARC]. This was originally located at Wesley's Chapel in City Road, London, but was transferred to Manchester in 1977. The archives contain over 26,000 printed records and several hundred thousand manuscripts, relating to all the branches of Methodism that existed before Methodist Union in 1932, as well as over 1300 items particularly relating to John Wesley. The Connexional records are of most help to researchers carrying out in-depth research on Methodism and to family and local historians who are interested in the history of a particular Chapel or Circuit. There are good collections of Methodist Chapel histories and Methodist newspapers and journals, which contain much biographical information about ministers, local preachers and prominent Methodist laymen. Other records include preaching plans, Methodist periodicals, Methodist fiction and obituaries.

It should be noted that **Methodist Connexional Records contain very little genealogical information.**

MARC also has complete sets of the Minutes of Conference of all the branches of Methodism. These have been published annually following each Conference since 1744, but their value to family historians is largely limited to the lists of stations of all ministers, active and retired, and detailed obituaries of ministers who have died since the last Conference.

Researchers are welcome to use the library facilities at John Rylands University Library but are advised to contact the Keeper of the Methodist Collections [Tel: 0161 834 5343]. A letter of reference and some form of identity is required for the first visit so that a Reader's Ticket can be issued.

N.B. John Rylands Library is closed for major refurbishment until 2006 during which time there is very limited access to the Methodist Connexional Records at Manchester University Library in Deansgate. Researchers are advised to telephone 0161 275 3751 before planning a visit, or visit the Manchester University Library website for the most up to date information on the refurbishment programme.

The Wesley and Methodist Studies Centre, based at Oxford Brookes University, houses the second most important printed collection relating to British Methodism. The Centre has a good collection of local histories, chapel histories, Methodist newspapers and journals and has the advantage of being within easy reach of the Midlands and Home Counties and, being a smaller centre, can offer a more personal service to visitors. It also houses the archives of Westminster College, which used to be a male teacher training college in Horseferry Road, Westminster. Visitors are welcome but prior booking is advised via the Methodist Heritage Co-ordinator, Wesley and Methodist Studies Centre, Westminster Institute of Education, Oxford Brookes University (see useful addresses on page 15).

Wesley's Chapel in City Road, London contains the Museum of Methodism in the crypt where many artefacts associated with John Wesley and early Methodist leaders can be seen. Next door is Wesley's House built at the same time as the Chapel. It was here that John Wesley slept when in London and also where he died on March 2nd 1791. Behind Wesley's Chapel is a Methodist Burial ground where John Wesley was buried on March 9th at 5a.m., 5,450 other burials took place here between 1799 and 1854. The Burial Registers have been transcribed and indexed by the London and North Middlesex Family History Society and are available for purchase in a set of four microfiche from the Society's Postal Sales Officer, Colin Gibbens, 1d Uplands Park Road, Enfield, Middlesex EN2 7PS. Tel: 020 8363 5516. UK price £3.95, including postage; overseas £4.90, including postage.

Across City Road from Wesley's Chapel is Bunhill Fields, a large Nonconformist burial ground containing the grave of Susannah Wesley, John Wesley's mother.

Englesea Brook, near Crewe in Cheshire, is the location for the Museum of Primitive Methodism. It houses the finest collection of British Primitive Methodist records. These include a large collection of PM Circuit plans listing ministers, local preachers and chapel officers; a Library of PM literature which includes bound copies of PM Magazines and a complete set of PM Minutes of Conferences from 1819-1932.

Englesea Brook is open from April to November on Thursdays, Fridays, Saturdays and Bank Holiday Mondays from 10.30am to 5.15pm each day and on Sundays from 1.30pm to 5.15pm. Visits at other times can be made by arrangement. There is a cottage with self-catering facilities nearby for visitors who wish to extend their research. Enquiries are welcome via the Warden [Tel: 01782 810109] or at the Museum [Tel: 01270 820836] or by e-mail engleseabrook-methodist-museum@supranet.com.

The New Room, John Wesley's Chapel in Broadmead, Bristol — is the oldest Methodist Chapel in the world. Built in 1739 it is open throughout the year on Mondays — Saturdays from 10.00am — 4.00pm each day. Further information can be obtained by telephoning 0117 926 4740. It does not contain much Methodist archival material.

The Family Records Centre holds a microfilm copy of the Wesleyan Methodist Metropolitan Registry which contains 10,341 baptismal certificates, which were registered at the Wesleyan Methodist Register Office, 66 Paternoster Row, near St Paul's Church, London between 1818 and 1840. There is an index — RG4/4680 and the certificates can be located in RG4/4677,4678 and 4679. This Registry is separate from the 856 Baptismal and Burial Registers that were surrendered to the Registrar General in 1840, which can also be seen at the FRC.

The British Library Newspaper Library at Colindale in North London, has extensive collections of Methodist newspapers including The Watchman [1835-1884], The Methodist Times [1885-1932], The Primitive Methodist [1868-1932], The Methodist Recorder [1861 to date], The Primitive Methodist Leader [1905-1925], The Methodist Leader [1926-1932], The Methodist Times and Leader [1932-1937], The Primitive Methodist World and Sunday School Worker [1883-1908].

The Archives at Methodist Central Hall Westminster in London contain the unique Wesleyan Methodist Historic Roll. This is a good starting off point to see if any of your ancestors may have been Wesleyan Methodists c.1900, provided you have a good idea where they were living at that time.

The Historic Roll comprises fifty large leather-bound volumes in which the names of more than 1,025,000 donors to the Wesleyan Methodist Twentieth Century Fund are recorded. Wesleyan Methodists and their friends were invited to donate one guinea (£1.05) and also make additional donations 'In Memoriam' for loved ones who had died or who had moved away from home. The Fund Raising Committee distributed special pages to every Wesleyan Chapel and Circuit in England, Wales, Scotland and overseas. Donors were asked to write their names and addresses on these pages which were returned to the Wesleyan Methodist Church offices in London and, after the Fund was finally closed in 1909, the 17,000 pages were bound into fifty volumes. The Twentieth Century Fund raised £1,073,682. £250,000 was allocated to purchase the site of the Royal Aquarium, opposite Westminster Abbey, and erect a building appropriate for a World Centre for Wesleyan Methodism — Central Hall Westminster. When the Hall was opened in 1912, the Historic Roll was placed in a specially constructed bookcase and made available for inspection by visitors.

In 2002, the Historic Roll was filmed and it is now possible for researchers to purchase microfiche copies of entries for a particular Wesleyan Chapel, Circuit or District, or to obtain photocopies of the pages showing the names of their family donors. Most donations were made between 1899 and 1904, so the names in the Historic Roll can, in many cases, be cross-referenced to the 1901 Census. Further information about the Historic Roll can be obtained via Visitor Services, Methodist Central Hall Westminster, Storey's Gate, Westminster, London SW1H 9NH or e-mail visitorservices@c-h-w.co.uk.

A typical entry in the Historic Roll.
Volume 2 p483 Clacton-on-Sea Circuit

Arthur Fitch	Brooklyn Villa, Church Road, Clacton-on-Sea
Mary Ann Fitch	ditto
Frank Fitch	ditto
Ernest Fitch	ditto

A more substantial entry on the same page

| Esther Cooke | In Memoriam |
| Mary Ann Cooke | Kent House, Peckham Rye, London |

In memory of Mark Cooke, who died in Didsbury College at the close of his third year in residence and was the first student who died there.

The entries for the Pearson Family in Volume 2 p339 Braintree (Essex) Wesleyan Chapel in the Chelmsford Circuit are particularly helpful to family history researchers.

Elizabeth Pearson	Ryde
Charles Pearson	In Memoriam
James Pearson	California
Charles John Pearson	Canada
Edward Bruce Pearson	Ryde
Nathaniel Pearson	In Memoriam
William Pearson	New South Wales
Joseph M Pearson	In Memoriam

The entries for the family of a Wesleyan Methodist Minister in Volume 41 p289 Horncastle Circuit also contain much family history

James Clegg, the late, Fairfield, Liverpool, son of Thomas Clague, Arragon Moor, Santon, Isle of Man.

Richard Clegg, eldest son of above, Wesley Chapel Liverpool, Wesleyan Minister, Stamford Circuit 1876.

James Whitehead Clegg, second son of above, Wesleyan Minister, Handsworth College 1886-9. Horncastle 1896-1899.

Mary Jane Clegg (nee Thompson) Keswick, Cumberland.

Percy Dixon Clegg, eldest son of Rev. J and Mrs Whitehead Clegg born at Ludlow Salop 1894.

Cyril Thompson Clegg second son, Rev. J and Mrs Whitehead Clegg born at Bromyard, Worcester 1896.

James Heber Clegg, third son of Rev. J and Mrs Whitehead Clegg, born at Horncastle 1898.

Eric Stanley Clegg, fourth son of Rev. J and Mrs Whitehead Clegg, born at Barton-on-Humber, 1900.

Nellie Pinkard and Rose Pinkard, Yeovil Somersetshire, twin sisters, maids to above.

12

METHODIST RECORDS IN SCOTLAND

The National Archives in Scotland holds an extensive collection of records of Wesleyan and Primitive Methodist Circuits and Synods in Scotland in Class CH11 dating from 1764 onwards.

The principal records comprise Circuit Minute Books, Baptismal Registers, Membership Lists, seat rents, Sunday School attendance, correspondence and miscellaneous papers, as well as Circuit plans, orders of service and published accounts. However, all Scottish Methodist Church records are closed for 30 years from the date of the last entry in that record. Records of a confidential nature are closed for 75 years from the date of the last entry in that record, unless permission has been granted to an individual in writing from the relevant Chapel or Circuit. Confidential records include disciplinary matters, complaints, statements of ministers and pastoral matters. A full list of deposited Methodist records can be found in the National Archives of Scotland website: www.nas.gov.uk. Copies of some 19th Century registers of Dunrossness and Lerwick in the Shetland Islands may be found at the Society of Genealogists.

METHODIST RECORDS IN WALES

A large number of Welsh Methodist Baptismal Registers were surrendered to the Registrar General in 1840. Microfilmed copies of these registers can be seen at the Family Records Centre in London, at the National Library of Wales, Aberystwyth, at County Record offices in Wales and at Family History Centres of the Church of Latter-Day Saints. Registers surrendered in 1840 include a large number of Calvinist Methodist Chapels, a small number of Wesleyan Methodist Chapels and Welsh Calvinist Chapels in the predominantly Welsh speaking counties of Cardiganshire and Merionethshire. Welsh Methodist Records after 1837 can be located in the National Library of Wales and in County Record Offices in Wales. Another source of information is Welsh Family History; A Guide to Research; edited by John and Sheila Rowlands (Second Edition 1998), which includes a chapter on Nonconformity by Muriel Bowen Evans.

OTHER IMPORTANT SOURCES

Hills' Arrangements – lists of Ministers and their stations compiled by Rev. William Hill in 1819 but updated to 1988. John Rylands University Library, Manchester.

The Circuits of Great Britain 1765 – 1885 compiled by Rev. Joseph Hall and since updated to 1980; also located at John Rylands University Library.

Ministers and Circuits of the Primitive Methodist Connexion – Rev. William Leary; published 1989 by Teamprint, Loughborough.

The United Methodist Church, Ministers and Circuits – Dr Oliver A Beckerlegge [1968]

Who's Who in Methodism, 1933: ministers and laymen in Methodism at the time of Methodist Union published by Methodist Times and Leader [Methodist Publications Ltd].

As an example of what you may find, the entry for Rev W E Sangster reads:

SANGSTER, William Edwin Robert, BA (London) born 1900 at London. Educated at Shoreditch Secondary School, London. Training College Handsworth and Richmond. Entered ministry 1922 (Wesleyan), married Margaret Conway of Ealing one son and one daughter. Circuits Liverpool (Bootle), Bognor Regis, Colwyn Bay, Liverpool (Bootle), Scarborough. Publications "Why Jesus never wrote a book", and many others. Special Interests golf and walking. Address: 21 Londesborough Road, Scarborough. Tel: Scarborough 1488.

The **Methodist Preachers' Who's Who, 1934** — names 25,000 preachers living at the time of publication, published by Shaw Publishing Company Ltd.

The entries for Edward Campion and Isaac Foot read:

CAMPION, Edward, born 1879 at Middle Rasen, Lincs. Educated at Elementary School. Married Emily Buckley one son, one daughter. Health Department Foreman. Local Preacher 1927 Newcastle-under-Lyme Circuit. Church offices held Sunday School Teacher, ex Sunday School Secretary (30 years). Public offices ex Rep. Late Wolstanton Utd U.D.C. (32 years). Winner of Triennial Certificate, Sunday School Teachers Exam 1903—1905. Present Address: Hillcrest, Liverpool Road, Cross Heath, Newcastle, Staffs.

FOOT, Isaac, M.P., born 1880 at Plymouth. Educated at Plymouth Public School and Hoe Grammar School. Married Eva Mackintosh five sons and two daughters. Solicitor. Local Preacher 1899 East Cornwall Mission Circuit. Circuit Offices ex Circuit Steward, Chairman of Executive, Temperance Council of Christian Churches, Chairman of Parliamentary Temperance Committee, Secretary for Mines 1931—32, Member of Plymouth Council 1907—22. Deputy Mayor of Plymouth 1921. Present address: Poncrebar, Callington, Cornwall, Tel: 21.

If you are still unsure where to locate Methodist records, contact the County Record Office nearest to the town or village where your ancestors lived after 1750. If they can't give you the answer, they can often refer you to a Methodist District Archivist or Circuit Archivist who may be able to help.

METHODIST RECORDS: A SELECT BIBLIOGRAPHY

Leary, William	My Ancestor was a Methodist	SOG 3rd Edition (1999)
Tabraham, Barrie	The Making of Methodism	Epworth Press (1995)
Shaw, Thomas	Methodist Guide to Cornwall	Methodist Publishing House (MPH)
Turner, John Munsey	Modern Methodism in England 1932—1998	Epworth Press (1998)
Leary, William and Vickers, John A	Methodist Guide to Lincolnshire and East Anglia	MPH
Idle, Christopher	The Journal of John Wesley (Abridged)	Lion Publishing (1986)
Edwards, John; Gentry, Peter; Thorne, Roger;	Methodist Guide to Bristol and the South West	MPH
Vickers, John and Young, Betty	Methodist Guide to London and the South East	MPH
Gordon, S Wakefield	John Wesley	Foundery Press (1990)
Greetham, Mary and Peter	Samuel Wesley of Epworth	Foundery Press (1990)
Vickers, John A	Charles Wesley	Foundery Press (1990)
Greetham, Mary	Susanna Wesley, Mother of Methodism	Foundery Press (1994)
Maser, Frederick E	The Wesley Sisters	Foundery Press (1990)
Topping, Mark	The New Room — John Wesley's Chapel, Bristol	Jarrold Publishing (2004)
	Wesley's Chapel	Pitkin Guide (2001)

Methodist Heritage — annually published booklet MPH or via the Methodist Heritage Convenor, 66 Besselsleigh Road, Wootton, Oxon OX13 6DX e-mail Methodist-heritage@forsaith-oxon.demon.co.uk.

USEFUL ADDRESSES: A SELECT LIST

The National Archives, Ruskin Avenue, Kew, Richmond, Surrey TW9 4DU. Tel: 020 8392 5200 e-mail: enquiry@nationalarchives.gov.uk.

Family Records Centre, 1 Myddelton Street, London EC1R 1UW. Tel: 020 8392 5300, e-mail: info@familyrecords.gov.uk.

British Library Newspaper Library, Colindale Avenue, London NW9 5HE. Tel: 020 7412 7353 e-mail: newspaper@bl.uk.

Genealogical Society of Utah, Hyde Park Family History Centre, 64-68 Exhibition Road, South Kensington, London SW7 2PA. Tel: 020 7589 8561. For details of Family History Centres in England and Wales. www.familysearch.org

National Archives of Scotland, HM General Register House, 2 Princes Street, Edinburgh, EH1 3YY. Tel: 0131 535 1334, e-mail: enquiries@nas.gov.uk

National Library of Wales, Penglais, Aberystwyth, SA23 3BU. Tel: 01970 632800, e-mail: holi@llgc.org.uk

Society of Genealogists Library, 14 Charterhouse Buildings, Goswell Road, London EC1M 7BA. Tel: 020 7251 8799, e-mail: library@sog.org.uk

Black Country Wednesbury Central Methodist Church Springhead, Wednesbury, West Midlands WS10 9AD. Contact Minister Tel: 01928 683 143 (holds a collection of books about Wednesbury Riots of 1743/4).

Epworth The Old Rectory, 1 Rectory Street, Epworth, near Doncaster, South Yorkshire DN9 1HX. e-mail curator@epwortholdrectory.org.uk

Halifax Mount Zion Methodist Church Upper Brockholes, Per Lane, Ogden, Halifax HX2 8X6. www.mountzionhalifax.org.uk Tel: 01422 844364. e-mail Irene.cunliffe@btopenworld.com

Manchester John Rylands University Library Methodist Archives, Oxford Road, Manchester M3 3EH. Http://rylibweb.man.ac.uk/data/dg/text/method.html Tel: 0161 834 5343 e-mail glloyd@fsl.ll.man.ac.uk

Methodist Central Hall Archives, Storey's Gate, London SW1H 9NH. www.c-h-w.com Tel: 020 7654 3825 or 3826. email: visitorservices@c-h-w.co.uk

Mow Cop The Chapel Museum Hillside, Chapel Bank, Mow Cop, Stoke-on-Trent ST7 3NA. Contact John Anderson Tel: 01782 522004.

Museum of Cornish Methodism Carharrack, Redruth, Cornwall TR16 5RB. Tel: 01209 820381 (for appointment to research its collection of Cornish Methodist History).

Museum of Methodism, Wesley's Chapel, 49 City Road, London EC1Y 1AU. www.wesleyschapel.org.uk Tel: 020 7253 2262.

Museum of Primitive Methodism, Englesea Brook, Crewe, Cheshire, CW2 5QW. www.engleseabrook-methodist-museum@supranet.com

Newcastle-upon-Tyne-Brunswick Methodist Church Brunswick Place, Newcastle-upon-Tyne NE1 7BJ. e-mail rev.terry@cwcom.net Tel: 0191 232 1692. Memorabilia available on request; prior appointment needed.

New Room (John Wesley's Chapel) Bristol, 36 The Horsefair, Bristol BS1 3JE. www.methodist.org.uk/new.room Tel: 0117 926 4740.

Wesley and Methodist Studies Centre, Oxford Westminster Institute of Education, Oxford Brookes University, Harcourt Hill, Oxford OX2 9AT. www.brookes.ac.uk/wco Tel: 01865 488286 e-mail wco@brookes.ac.uk

Wesley College, Bristol, College Park Drive, Henbury Road, Bristol BS10 7QD. e-mail admin@wesley-college-bristol.ac.uk (Contains a Library of Wesleyana pre 1851 books).

SPECIALIST METHODIST BOOKSELLERS

Methodist Publishing House, 4 John Wesley Road, Werrington, Peterborough PE4 6ZA, Tel: 01733 325002, website: www.mph.org.uk.

Gage Postal Books, PO Box 105, Westcliff-on-Sea, Essex SS0 8EQ, Tel: 01702 715133, e-mail: gagebooks@clara.net

Alan Rose Books, 26 Roe Cross Green, Mottram, Hyde, Cheshire SK14 6LP, Tel: 01457 763485

METHODIST CALENDAR

1703 [June 17] Birth of John Wesley at Epworth, Lincolnshire

1725 [September 25] John Wesley ordained deacon in Anglican Church

1726 [March 17] John Wesley elected Fellow of Lincoln College, Oxford

1729 Methodist Society formed at Oxford University

1735 [October] John Wesley sailed for Georgia

1738 [February 1] John Wesley lands at Deal after turbulent time in Georgia

1738 [May 24] John Wesley's Aldersgate Street conversion

1739 [April 2] John Wesley's first open air sermon in Bristol

1739 [June 5] New Room, Bristol open for public worship

1739 [November] Foundery Chapel in Moorfields, London opened

1744 First Methodist Conference

1748 [June 24] John Wesley opened Kingswood School in Bristol

1760s First overseas Methodists in Antigua and America

1769 First preachers volunteer to go to America

1778 [January] Armenian Magazine launched

1778 [November] Opening of Wesley's Chapel in City Road

1779 [August] First Conference held in the new Chapel

1780 New Methodist Hymn Book published

1784 Thomas Coke's first missionary appeal

1784 First Ordinations

1786 First missionaries sent to West Indies

1788 [March 29] Death of Charles Wesley

1790 [October 6] John Wesley's last open air sermon at Winchelsea

1791 [February 23] John Wesley's last sermon at Leatherhead

1791 [March 2] Death of John Wesley

1797 Methodist New Connexion founded

1807 Primitive Methodist Connexion founded

1812 Woodhouse Grove School founded

1814 First Missionaries sent to Asia

1815 Bible Christians founded

1815 First Missionaries sent to Australia

1818 Wesleyan Missionary Society founded

1827 The Leeds Organ case — Protestant Methodist Connexion founded

1834 Beginning of Ministerial training

1834 Wesleyan Methodist Association founded

1834 Tolpuddle Martyrs

1857 United Methodist Free Church formed

1907 United Methodist Church formed

1912 [October 3rd] Methodist Central Hall Westminster opened.

1932 The Methodist Church formed with the coming together of United Methodist, Primitive Methodist and Wesleyan Methodist Churches.